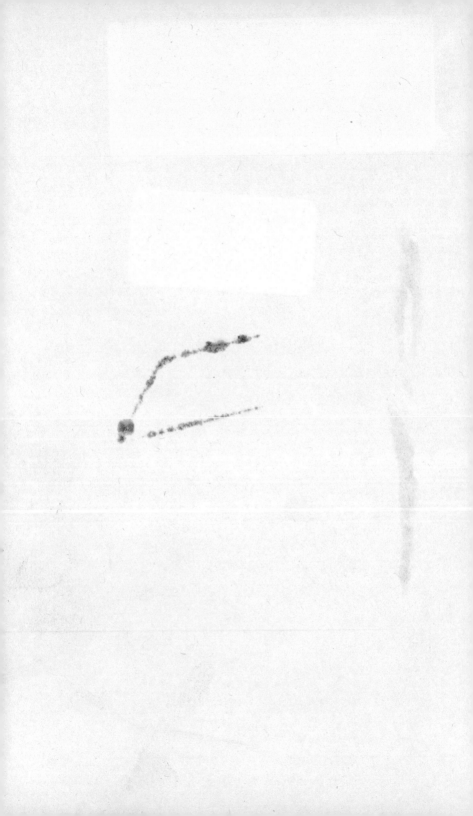

THE ROAD
TO OXFORD

A. L. ROWSE

THE ROAD TO OXFORD

The past is for poets, the present for pigs — SAMUEL PALMER

JONATHAN CAPE
THIRTY BEDFORD SQUARE LONDON

First published 1978
© A. L. Rowse 1978

Jonathan Cape Ltd, 30 Bedford Square, London WC1

British Library Cataloguing in Publication Data

Rowse, Alfred Leslie
The Road to Oxford
I. Title
821'.9'12   PR6035.084

ISBN 0–224–01573–7

Printed in Great Britain by
Cox and Wyman Ltd
London, Fakenham and Reading

For
Eleanor Longfellow Brewster

Contents

Preface

He is a bold man who dares to publish a volume of poems today. In no department of literature is the confusion and breakdown of standards more apparent. It is true that in the revolution that is undermining traditional, civilised society, landmarks are being removed in all the arts: music, painting, sculpture, as well as literature. One consequence is that people are unable to tell the authentic from the bogus. Another is the deplorable state of criticism, which gives them no help but adds to the confusion, when it does not contribute to the decline, sets up false values, and patronises inferior verse, not the less pretentious for hardly being verse, let alone poetry.

What is the honest, the real artist to do, with the traditional world of art breaking down all round him, along with the society which nourished it?

We can see from the experience of countries which have undergone shattering revolution, like Soviet Russia, where a true poet such as Akhmatova was unable to publish her poems for twenty years. In countries where the social revolution is less flagrant, the censorship is more occult, the patronage of official bodies less obtrusive, the cultivation of what conforms hardly less cynical, when it is not just unintelligent, intellectually third-rate.

We may take courage from the fact that the true artist, whether painter or poet, works for himself alone, while welcoming those elect spirits who can feel and think along with him – no matter what nonsense prevails or is promoted by a mass-society 'without pride of ancestry or hope of posterity'.

Independence Day,   A. L. Rowse
1977

November Sunrise

RUSSET and rusty and gold,
   The trees look wintry and old –
Though it is early November,
A month away from December.

Below the window I see
A contrast in greenery:
Puffs of perennial leaves
In mounded and rounded sheaves.

To me within the room
Reaches the muffled hum,
The mysterious harmony
Of the further, outer sea.

Or is it the inner caves
The quiet water laves,
Making a secret sound,
A music underground?

The eastern sky, ice-blue,
Now flushes a rosy hue,
And dawn announces the day
Over the sleeping bay.

Between me and the sea
A screen of filigree:
Dark and skeletal trees
Erect a formal frieze:

Through which an orange sun,
Curtains of night withdrawn,
Rises over the bay
Triumphant – and it is day.

Winter at Trenarren

WINTER howls at the window,
    The trees are all distressed;
In the east an angry sunrise,
    Clouds pile up in the west.

Summer, alas, is over
    With all its gallant days:
Moorland and headland and meadow
    With bright sun ablaze.

Clouds gather over the landscape,
    The wind howls like a wolf;
Draw the curtains closer,
    The rafters shake in the roof.

Light the silver candles,
    Poke the glowing fire,
Where the fallen timber
    Makes the flames leap higher.

Bring my books about me,
    Take them down from the wall,
Stack them all around me,
    Buttressed against a fall.

Make my chair a refuge
    From the winter's rage,
And all the room a fortress,
    Firelit, from old age.

The Ancient House

THE night is full of noises, false alarms –
O preserve me from its harms –
A summer wasp awakes from winter sleep,
Drowsily explores the hanging at my head;
Bed creaks, door bangs at the far back,
A dull thud among rafters of the roof.
The ancient house, demure and coy by day,
Lovely and withdrawn, reserving her secret,
By night comes alive, to live once more
Her life of the past, respond to footfalls
Of former habitants, answer their muffled calls
For consolation and relief, in suffering,
The awakening of those born and those who died.
This secret life of stifled noises
Like scuttlings of mouse or bat or rat
Warns me of my end in turn
Among all those.
Perhaps the footfall I hear upon the stair
Is my predestined murderer:
Already there.

Winter Splendour

Bands of orange and blue
    One sees the black trees through –
Now gold amid the dun
Lit by the risen sun.

And brighter lemon below
Burns an improbable glow –
O saisons! O châteaux!

Season of delight –
Winter, when lawns are white:

A filigree of trees,
What brushwork dark, Chinese,
More delicate than these?
Moon and attendant star,
Venus or Jupiter,
Keep watch the white house over
Against what ghosts may hover,
Unearthly light distil
Over sea and hill:

Reign supreme in the sky,
While here at last I lie
Watching the fire's red eye.

Outside, the radiant night
A silver splendour of light –
O world beyond all thought,
O universe unsought,
Before my fire goes out.

Native Sky

ST Mabyn church-tower tops the world,
In the south the woods of Pencarrow,
Clouds dapple the valley to St Kew;
In the field, tractor and harrow.

The farmboy whistles as he goes
Making his tracks across;
A white gull follows his dark shadow;
We sit by the wayside cross.

From the granite steps five churches appear:
St Endellion peeps a pinnacle.
St Eval punctuates the west,
St Minver spires the hill.

Stockinged cattle crop the stubble;
Above, the barrow's edge;
Afternoon sun on the face of St Kew,
A pheasant calls in the hedge.

A signpost points to St Endellion,
Chapel Amble, Wadebridge;
The gulls rise soundless from the loam,
Toadflax glints on the ledge.

The sleeping farms lie all around,
And never shall you and I
Meet this magic moment again
Under our native sky.

End of Day

THE sun sets behind Helman Tor
  As I journey on my way –
Bradock church, Boconnoc woods –
Home from the delights of day:

Castle Drogo on its height,
With half of Dartmoor all around,
Mortonhampstead, the Dart at Postbridge,
A distant view of Plymouth Sound.

Across the Tamar are the places
Chiefly beloved: Couch's[1] Mill,
Lerryn, Lansallos, St Winnow church,
Restormel keep upon its hill.

These I have known since I was a child –
Sunrise and sunset, they keep me still
Company: Boconnoc and Lerryn,
The river Fowey and Couch's Mill.

These are the names upon my heart
As I journey on my way,
And sun sets behind Helman Tor,
Homeward at the end of day.

[1] Pronounced Cooch; the word means red.

Helman Tor

A BUZZARD circles Helman Tor:
The prehistoric monster lours –
Saurian or pterodactyl –
Through an eternity of hours

Over its own intrinsic moor.
The mottled cattle crop below,
The stunted thorns creep up the flanks
And sharp their crippled shadows show,

Over the hill the pinnacles
Of Lanlivery church stick animal ears
Into the sky – as at any time
Since down the valley the Cavaliers,

From Stratton Hill to Bradock Down,
Crashed their way to final defeat.
Boulders upheave like elephant rumps,
Grey and wrinkled, out of the peat.

Beyond, the tiny patterned fields,
While overhead the buzzard planes;
Kingdoms are lost and empires fall,
States decay. But this remains.

Easter at St Enodoc

for Anne Mathias

O Mably and Treverton and Guy,
   Here at St Enodoc they lie
Together beneath the twisted spire,
Across from Stepper and Pentire:

There runs the blue crystalline sea
Beyond the open estuary,
Where breaks the line of surf and spray
On the Doom Bar of Padstow Bay.

Tamarisk shrouds the church around:
There's the quarry whence came the stone,
Many a headstone on its mound
Lit at night by the light from Trevone.

Here a seaman cast on shore,
Far from the home his footsteps trod,
Nameless, alone, in time of war:
'Unknown to us, but known to God.'

Easter has garnished the graves with flowers
Placed by many a friendly hand;
Tumulus clouds and late March showers
Threaten across the shadowed land.

Up the lane the poet lives,
Flowering currant at his door:
Inspiration receives, and gives,
From hill and valley, stream and shore.

Within the church the candles are lit,
Flicker upon the upturned faces,
Where the assembled parish sit
In their accustomed pews and places.

Spring flowers brighten sill and pew,
Put about by the faithful few;
From the west a transient gleam
Upon the figures rapt in dream:

The western window says, bright and clear,
'He is risen. He is not here.'
Scent of grass and Easter sun,
Service is over and day is done.

Demelza

A MILE long lane to Demelza,
    Half a mile to Great Bryn:
At the end of it shall I find the old folk
    In the lonely farm they were in?

The vast hearth open to the sky,
    A wisp of smoke thin and grey,
An ingle-nook you sit inside,
    Look up and see the blue of day.

The midday meal is being cooked
    In the middle of the afternoon,
In a fine muddle of flour and flurry,
    Hands in the dough without a spoon;

Potato peelings and bits and pieces
    Litter table and floor and chair,
Roof and rafters hung with oddments;
    The door opens, and suddenly there

Stand widowed farmer, and son
    A natural, courteous and kind:
This their ancestral place beneath
    The ancient camp, time out of mind.

These are the last of the family –
    What will become of it and them,
Failing and faltering to their end?
    No one to succeed, nothing to stem

The slow and steady onset of time
    In this queer sequestered place,
Surrounded by fallen walls and ghosts:
    The end of their familiar race,

Who built their own chapel by the road,
    Tended by the faithful band,
Now down to these last, of all the ghosts
    On whom John Wesley laid his hand.

The Monoliths

HIGH up on St Breoke Downs
   Stand those very ancient stones
Of ominous, forbidding shape,
Erect amid recumbent sheep.

Slightly leaning to each other,
Braving every wind and weather
They loom, sulking and solitary,
On prehistoric cemetery;

Between, the breast-heave of a mound
Dominating miles around.
On close-cropped grass and nibbled pasture
They keep their ceremonious posture.

One confronts the rising sun,
The other the west, when day is done.
A farmer, from a wooded dell
Mysterious as Marinel,

Emerges in this lonely place,
Copper-coloured, louring face,
Attendant on the spirits here,
Fancies he sees a human leer

Across the taller standing stone
When day lifts at winter dawn,
And fires are lit on Midsummer night,
Setting the beacon all alight.

For then the centuries fall away
In the glare of night turned into day,
Recall the sacrificial rites
That filled with horror the lurid nights.

The bonfires burning were fires of bones
Burnt at the foot of the standing stones;
The people lacerate with rods
Their manic selves. These were their gods.

St Clement's

A GAP in the hedge, a grey church tower
       Backed by the blue of a river –
St Clement's lies on a tongue of land
       Where the Fal flows on for ever.

The grey tower stands in a sea of blue,
       Honeyed light of noon
On lichened face and buttressed grace;
       In the sky a wisp of moon.

Two white cottages for sale
       The pretty place discloses,
Climbed all over by clematis;
       In the garden, roses.

The church gate opens upon the graves,
       Berberis, ivy and moss;
The gravel path leads down to the porch,
       Below stands Ignioc's Cross.

We push the door and enter the aisle –
       Coloured lights of glass –
Read the monuments on the wall;
       Shadows pass and re-pass.

But whose tall shade comes down the path
       From Penmount high on its hill?
The friend of my youth, whose parish this was:
       The place remembers him still.

Summer Work

THERE'S a touch of autumn in the trees today,
     A fringe of gold in the serrated leaves
Of Trenarren beeches along the upper path.
All summer long the groups and families
Have drifted by the hedge in twos and threes
To picnic and copulate at Ropehawn, Hallane,
In coves and caves out on the headland,
While I, stripped to the waist, cope with weeds,
Thistles, docks, couch-grass, uncut hedges,
In August heat of the valley open to the sea.
Overgrown orchard unpruned, dropping fruit
For unhived honey-bees and wasps to eat:
The drones of the people have no will to work.
Hook or scythe in hand I watch them pass,
Contempt in my eyes that meet their gaze:
For consolation when I turn my back
Cloudless blue over V-shaped valley,
Fountains of fuchsias, dripping crimson rain
Over the lane, where old Ben the bull
Used to come swinging home. No longer now.
A sudden scent of aromatic pine
Comes from the spinney, and over all
The summer gale from smouldering sea
Makes a hive-like murmur from the bay
Brimming with phosphorescent ecstasy
Out to the horizon: the valley filled with a voice
Wordless, the language of dreams and sleep,
Undertow, undertone, a burden of content.

Kenwyn Bells

for Elly Noon

O KENWYN bells! the sound that dwells
    Long after in the ear,
Coming down the vale of Allen,
    Silvery and clear:

When on the hill-top of Penmount
    We were still together,
On summer Sundays of the past
    The chimes ran down the river;

By Killagordon and Ventongimps,
    And outwards to Polwhele,
Past Clement's Cross and Penair Turn
    On to Little Penheale.

Beside the tower the bishops kept
    Their vigil at their ease –
Lis Escop in its hillside garden,
    Ensconced among the trees.

Time has dispersed us all who then
    Had not yet left our home,
And he who lent it mirth and life
    Lies in his grave in Rome.

Bodmin Moor

I USED to go this way to Oxford,
    Past Penstroda and Trethorne,
On such a day at end of summer,
    A grey and clouded September morn.

The moorland ponies crop the turf,
    The sheep are strewn across the moor,
Grey and immobile as rocks
    From prehistoric ocean floor.

The signposts point to Blisland, Temple,
    St Neot, Cardinham farther away,
Through Bolventor and by Dozmary:
    Bursts of gorse light up the way.

Sunflowers in a cottage garden
    Turn their dials to the south;
A clapper bridge crosses the river
    Where herons rise from the undergrowth.

Perched on the shoulder of Rowtor
    St Michael's chapel guards the height:
A rainbow fills the threatening sky
    With fragile momentary light.

Sudden showers cross the moorland,
    Sunshine, blue sky and mingled rain:
April weather – but this is autumn,
    And not for me comes spring again.

Oxford beckoned at end of journey
    With youth and friends much to my mind:
The rain beats down, the moor is dark
    With advancing clouds, and life's behind.

Yarcombe Hill

On Yarcombe Hill the birds sing shrill
      While Geoffrey and I toil on our way;
The road winds steeply down to the bridge.
      And all is glad on a summer's day.

We look across the heave of the hill
      Where Sheafhayne manor secret lies:
Ransomed by Drake with Spanish gold
      Captured beneath Pacific skies;

Lived in still by the family's
      Descendant, a young Guards' officer,
Returned from the war to continue the line,
      Francis Drake's last, ultimate heir.

On Yarcombe Hill the wind blows cold
      Across the valley from Sheafhayne;
Down the path and in at the porch
      Alone I shelter from autumn rain.

The wind blusters around the church,
      The half-hour bursts upon the chime;
Within, I pace the aisle and mark
      The monuments of former time.

Near the altar I note the tablet
      To the young soldier's memory –
Already inscribed ten years ago:
      'He liveth in eternity.'

All around the saints stand still,
      St James with staff and scallop-shell,
St Peter with his key, St John,
      The Virgin in her tabernacle.

On Yarcombe Hill the snow lies thick
    Upon the silent winter slopes,
All down to where the River Yarty
    Dark under frozen surface sleeps.

Turning to go, behind me the gate
    Clangs above my muffled tread,
Awakes me, Geoffrey, from my dream:
    I cannot remember you are dead.

Marytavy

for John Betjeman's seventieth birthday

M ARYTAVY, Marytavy,
  Blinking in the August sun,
We draw up at the churchyard gate
  After a Sunday morning run,

Up the valley from Tavistock,
  Skirting the edges of the Moor –
No one for church at Petertavy,
  Silent the bells and locked the door.

On we go around the gorge
  Over the narrow bridge we slow:
A couple of fishermen at the weir –
  This summer's drouth the water's low.

And all around is spiritual drouth,
  Nonconformity in Devon
Dried up, the Methodist chapel shut:
  No one to go that way to Heaven.

And what shall we find at Marytavy?
  Apprehensively we search
Up the path and in at the porch –
  To find the parish all in church.

Six candles flare upon the altar,
  There all dressed in ferial green,
Out from the vestry pops the priest,
  Biretta and chasuble brightly seen;

Shuffling behind his acolytes two,
  Spectacles on the tip of his nose.
Under the roodscreen, into the chancel
  And up the altar steps he goes.

All three genuflect together,
    He takes the incense-boat in hand,
Gives the altar a thorough censing,
    While very reverently we stand;

And all the parish sings the Mass
    In plainchant to the manner born,
The *Gloria* first: it's all as if
    The Reformation had never been.

Here on the western slopes of Dartmoor
    The incense mingles with morning air:
Lost in thought, I lose my place,
    Look up, and see the priest is there,

Coming down the aisle, with flick of wrist
    Besprinkles the folk with holy water;
Unaccustomed, to my suprise,
    I suddenly receive a spatter.

Unexpectedly sanctified,
    Rather abashed, we beat a retreat;
The Mass goes on, but all around
    At Marytavy the air is sweet.

The Road to Ken

TURNING down the road to Ken,
What should I discover then?
An unknown road, a secret lane:
Shall I ever come this way again?

Above the path a rose-red tower,
On the face of the church-clock the hour:
The gilt hands tell a-quarter-to-ten
To the good people of the parish of Ken.

All on a still September morn
When from the fields the harvest's shorn,
A rose-red tower in a churchyard green
Roots in the inner mind the scene,

Gives something to remember when
I'm far from Devon and the fields of Ken.

Up in the clouds, approaching Maine,
The scene comes back in mind again:
The harvest home, the carts in shed,
The church-tower rooted in the dead.

A world away, and I wonder when
I'll see again the lane to Ken?

The Bewitched Woman

THE bewitched woman – she was beautiful once:
    What can have happened that she got like this?
Wandering around the great house like one lost,
Living all alone, the furniture piled up,
A maze of paths through which to thread one's way,
Brown paper on the floor, no carpet laid,
No curtains or hangings to keep out the sun,
Nor east wind funnelling up the valley.
Behold the swept gravel, the blue hydrangeas –
You'd not believe the devastation within:
Packing-cases unopened after years,
Every piece of tissue paper treasured
To harbour the unswept dust. Nobody comes
To pay a visit, or clean, or cook a meal:
'When I'm on my own, I don't bother.'
She's always on her own, wandering
From precious object to object, laying a hand
On things into which her life has drained and lost
All meaning and coherence. Each thing becomes
An end in itself: an oriental jade-tree,
A lacquer tray, a piece of amethyst;
Or hoarding the locks of ancestral hair,
Flaxen, gold, auburn, chestnut, grey,
Of haughty Pitts and querulous Grenvilles,
The pistols of a homicidal peer,
Who died in a duel – herself as mad as they.
How to account for it? Married to a man
Tepid and impotent, for money and rank,
Love already given to a shooting tough –
See on the chimney-piece his photograph,
All tweeds and knickerbockers of the twenties,
Broad-shouldered, broad-bottomed, affable

And male: he would have fathered a family
Drowned now in the depths of her angry eyes.
The bland and circumspect Queen Anne façade
Gives no hint of the disordered dream within,
The chaos of a ruined mind, the heart
Frozen and empty, the red and roughened hands
That once were fine, enamelled and beringed,
For ever flickering over the stored Sèvres,
Branches of crystal, bowls of golden agate
That, afternoons, hold the honeyed light.
Dust accumulates upon the Hepplewhite
And Sheraton; upon the ormolu table
A cake consumed by spiders – it might be
Miss Haversham's bridal cake preserved for tea.

The hours wear on in this house fallen asleep,
No difference made between night and morn,
The shutters never shut, blinds undrawn,
A sad enchantment spun about it all.
What will be the end of it? I see
Some chance marauder stealthily mount the stair,
Shuffling along the crowded corridor –
And the shed blood upon the cracked mirror.
Or perhaps a quieter end may supervene
In the tumbled bed that never has been made,
A havering light peer in upon the scene
Through cobwebbed windows of the moonlit front
Looking down the valley to lovely Lerryn,
The bridge, the boats that beckon to the open sea.

Boconnoc

I AM haunted by the thought of beautiful Boconnoc
   In all the tenderness of spring:
Golden glades of daffodils beneath the beeches,
Antlered heads of stags well down in bracken,
The aspiring obelisk, the church and King Charles
Sleeping in his coach: all the memories of 1644.
Yet it's not that that possesses me,
But the southward slope where that sad couple
Are now together. I am haunted by the insatisfaction
Of their lives: the grand Abbey wedding,
The beauty of Dropmore and Boconnoc,
Surrounded by tenantry, obsequious
To those out-of-date grandees. Leftovers
From Victorian days: the eccentric state,
Though with hardly a servant to mitigate
Their *tête-à-tête*,which they would punctuate
With improbable journeys to Peru or up the Nile.
Nothing to say to each other through decades.
No children. No family life. Nothing to enjoy
Save the surrounding silence of park,
Rides of rhododendrons, cliff of rock-garden
Variegated with every kind of erica in bloom,
Sweet-scented azalea and broom.
From the church above I looked down on him
Below, moving slowly along the terrace
To the Chinese garden seats, for a breath of air,
Having spent half a sad lifetime there.
Now she comes to join him, remote lady
With the hot and angry eyes,
Never having known what it was to live;
Keeping tryst with the dusty treasures,
Bric-à-brac, bibelots, piles of Sèvres,

Disjecta membra of the Grenvilles and the Pitts,
The busts of the forbears: no thought for successors.

I am obsessed by the mystery of people's lives,
The mingled unhappiness and beauty,
The coldness and courtesy, the ritual and duty
Where there is no love.
Only the memories when days were full
Of observances and routine, attendants,
Butlers and footmen, maids, keepers,
Shooting parties over the coverts:
All dwindling down to a lonely couple,
Beds unmade, stale food untasted –
The wide domain unchanged around them,
The blank windows of the long gallery
Looking down the valley of the Lerryn,
Spreading oaks and beeches,
Plash of unregarding fountain,
The circumference of park around
That sheltered slope, the grave
Open to the sun.

The Devil from Linkinhorne

*'The ordinary aspects of daily life prove to be of no great
fictional interest.'* Flannery O'Connor

The Devil was born in Linkinhorne, they say:
I knew him in the village as a boy: he lived next door.
He came to St Austell as a navvy on the line.
He didn't drink, everything with him was sex.
A wonderful way he had with animals,
Birds and snakes, fitches and ferrets and women:
Reptiles, dogs and bitches would alike respond.
I've seen him take a maggot out of a sick
Ferret's neck not daring to bite the hand
That held the writhing whip of steel by the throat,
And cure the beast. He had a magic thumb.
Out of his pocket with no trouble he'd take
A coiling adder and make it comfortable,
Himself bite off the tender tail of a mongrel.
'I worship the ground he treads on,' said one hot woman,
Panting uphill from Holmbush to Tregonissey:
All the women but Jane, who could not hold him –
His wife, who had no imagination for him.

She had been warned about him, but too late:
A piece of lard enabled him to enter –
She found herself pregnant, poor simple fool –
People in those days knew not what to do.
Her godly parents shocked, her pious father
Sat up in bed at night to read the Bible
By a candle to the assembled family
With all the lengthened -èds of Holy Writ,
Spectacles on nose. What good did it do?

Lena Grose at Weighbridge, his fancy woman,
He'd spend the weekends there in bed with her,
Leaving his children in the village to starve,
Not a penny in the house for Jane,
Honest and afraid of him, shining and clean.
What was there about him? The magnetic look
In the eyes, cold and cruel, with no kindness —
Quite young he was a cynic about people,
Knew himself, and thought no better of others.
There was the ivory skin, the pure pallor,
Refinement of line upon sensuous features,
A profile could have gone upon a coin,
The well-cut lips with their upturn of scorn.

Innocent then, I never noticed the curve
In the leathern breeches, masculine and taut.
One day there he bared his chest of hair
Curly and golden, to affront and shock
The priggish boy, showed him a wooden phallus
He had carved, red-tipped and lipped as a rose,
For his erotic purposes.
                                        What a gift
He had for growing roses, grafting stolen
Shoots upon wild briar; for making a garden —
With hidden garden-seat for fumbling girls,
The sleepers thieved, brought home by night from
        the line.
What a talent for bush-beating and liming birds:
The court was full of the song of captured
And caged finches, and there'd be a canary or two —
Seeds for them, if no food for the family.
He usually carried a net in his pocket,

Nor failed to mark the run of rabbit or hare –
There'd be a feed next door when we were asleep,
The feathers of plucked pheasant to tell the tale;
While old Cornelius, the crone with witch's chin,
From behind her blind would look balefully on,
Curse and ill-wish him as she did all men,
Having been early deserted with children
By her man – lost somewhere now in America.

He'd steal anything he could lay hand on –
My mother's scrubbing brush left in a bush
By the door, although she was feeding his young:
What did he care? He knew that for all her air
Of being superior she was only a woman,
Flung a four-letter word in her face: she flinched,
Hung back – 'You know very well what it means.'
She did: she shrunk away like one whipped.
He had respect for neither God nor woman.
For him they were all Eve, he their snake.
When war came, he was a malingerer,
They never knew where to find a fly-by-night.
Then, run to earth, he hung his chest and legs
Heavy with coppers and keys to induce symptoms
Of varicose veins and swallowed pieces of soap
To fabricate foam at the mouth, affect the heart,
When called up for military service.
Rejected, he was sent to make munitions
In Limehouse. The life of the East End in wartime,
Neglect of himself, perhaps the prostitutes,
Killed him, who was a natural pagan,
A denizen of country woods and fields.

Still a young man only in his thirties,
A shadow of himself, he came home to die
With his little son, his victim, who took his disease:
Both of them tended faithfully to the last
In the stricken court – no birdsong or roses now –
By mute and patient, uncomprehending Jane.

Winter Is Here

M Y life is folding up, leaf by leaf:
First one petal, then another is shed.
I can no longer walk around the garden,
Let alone take tool as once I could,
Hoe and fork on shoulders, shears under arm,
Sally down the stony path to paddock,
For a day's work on border, plot and bed,
The skies of Trenarren wheeling overhead.
Nor take the scythe and rake to tennis-court,
An overgrown wilderness when I
Come home from Oxford in July. No more
Climb up into the rafters of the roof
And out upon the leads, to view the valley,
Green slopes descending to the sparkling sea.
An old man on a stick hobbles round
Terrace and level lawn outside the house:
No more those day-long tramps across the moor,
Up the white and glistening granite roads
To Trethurgy – the otter's hamlet – and Luxulyan,
On through ferny brakes to Lanlivery,
The church-tower rising suddenly on the right,
And down into Lostwithiel, my head full
Of Richard, King of the Romans, the Black Prince,
And all their train sweeping up by the river
To the grey walls of Restormel on its hill.
Or in later years to visit my old friends
At lordly Lanhydrock – myself now old as they
Remaining in the cool and shadowy house,
While we walked up the sloping lawns to see
The magnolias hold their torches to the sun,
Rare rhododendrons and scented azaleas.
No longer scramble down the rocks to the beach

Ar Hallane, past Will Treleaven's flower-fields,
The red and showering fuchsias, the strawberry beds,
To slip into ice-cold water beneath the stream.
The summers are gone, spring and even autumn:
The sere winter of life is here, is here.

To Oxford

THROUGH early Sunday sleep of Biscovèy,
 Not disturbing the sleep of my grandparents
Nearby in the churchyard, from whose seed I stem:
I pass the church at St Blazey, lights at the altar,
The celibate priest saying his early Mass.
Lovely Luxulyan Valley of my youth
Opens its mouth to the waterfall, leads up
To the claypits, my poor father's industry.
A rook in the road, black-coated clergyman,
Rises and flaps into the fields of Penknight,
Of my ancient neighbours, the Kendalls of Pelyn.
Clematis climbs the wall at No Man's Land;
Irises flag a garden, bluebells in the hedges
And dandelion clocks, the flowers over.
Lostwithiel, the Duchy stannary town
In its hollow, is still asleep. No smoke rises,
But azaleas and rhodos fume upon the walls;
Loveliest of trees, the cherry now explodes
In suburban pink along the bough. Princely
Boconnoc of the Pitts and Fortescues
Spreads its woods upon the skyline towards Looe.
The turning to Lanhydrock takes me in thought
To the grey mansion, nested among trees,
The last of the family sitting out their days
In their redoubt between church and barbican;
The avenue planted in the Commonwealth time
By that stern Puritan, the Lord Robartes,
So past Catchfrench, of kind George Brimmacombe,
Lived there complete with boy-friend and a wife.
Now the high moors – Caradon, Kit Hill – open
Out towards Dartmoor: I prepare to cross the Tamar.

All on a May morning memories throng:
Charles long dead, Richard and Bruce dead,
Geoffrey now dead, my early dearest friends –
I take the road to Oxford now alone.

Oxford Station

SEE that man standing on the platform
  Hat in hand, west wind in his hair,
Back to the passengers waiting for the train,
A look of some disdain for the nondescripts,
Ruffling squalid newspapers, chewing,
Chattering and shacking up with each other,
Acne'd girls and pimpled, graceless youths:
All the *tohu-bohu* of Eastern Europe,
And odds and ends from Asia, Africa.
Impatiently he awaits the signal
When a cat cautiously crosses the track:
He is alarmed for an animal
Self-contained and lithe, beautiful and free.
An engine approaches, across the breast-plate
OMOO – he recognises the signal
From a fellow-spirit, Melville,
Restless and ranging, like himself
Unrecognised by the herd, solitary
And free.

Trowbridge

SENDING a book to California
      I notice upon the fly-leaf these few words:
'To John, from Mother' – sometime in the twenties.
The book, old Farnell of Exeter's
An Oxonian Looks Back, proud book-plate
Of the young owner, of *Coll: Exon: Oxon.*
There's the high gable of the Sainte Chapelle
The Victorians imitated in their day,
A college room facing away down Ship Street.
Here he lived his quiet life in the twenties,
A sober exhibitioner, a barber's son,
Yellow corn-coloured hair, long of leg,
Like Edward Longshanks with one drooping eyelid –
A curious effect of collusion it gave.
How proud Mother must have been of her lanky son,
Who had won an exhibition to come to Oxford.

This look into the past in a faded book
Opened a gate in the wall, the years now dead
When spring thrilled along the nerves and veins:
In summer those shadowy watered streets,
The Turl, the Broad and Brasenose Lane,
The life so hurriedly lived, so much enjoyed,
And now all over, folded and put away.
The later schoolmaster, talented with boys,
Rumpling their hair, producing them in plays,
The affectation of professional theatre-chat,
With mumbled, half-articulated speech;
The summer conferences organised at Stratford,
Cosy rooms reserved at the Swans' Nest
Looking on the river, Hugh Clopton's bridge.
He had more fun than I with likely friends,

A gleam of expectation in tolerant eyes
Blue as his distant Wiltshire downs and skies.

Today I came through Trowbridge on my way
To Oxford, and wondered where was the barber's shop
Vanished these many years and where lived the boy
Who walked across fields to Hilperton and Melksham,
The church-bells of Wiltshire in his ears.
Over the town hung the smell of brewing hops,
Young folk scurrying here and there, as if
He might be one, a life now over and done.
Prunus and cherry white along the bough,
Cushions of arabis adhering to the wall,
Aubrietia blue and bursts of forsythia
In little terraced gardens – I wonder where
They lived, the barber's family now extinct,
Mother's son not one for marrying,
And only I to remember him passing by.

'The Revenant'

THE door opens to the familiar key,
And once more I am within the rooms
Formerly my own, no longer mine.
I am a stranger. Yet so much of life
Passed within these walls, so much
Happiness in work, looking up to see
Gold and black caverns in the copper beech,
The rose-flush of dawn upon the Camera,
Moonlight upon the dome sifted with snow.
So much, too, of anguish and waiting –
Waiting for whom, or what? I will not say.
My feet echo along the empty corridor,
Here are the bookshelves that held my books,
The gaping windows that leave too much exposed –
The familiar ghost, the unwanted *revenant*.
The floorboards quicken to my faithful feet,
Send back an unacquainted sound.
Nothing has changed. Yet all has changed:
Some spirit has flown, gone out of things,
Leaving untouched only a glimpse of the garden
From my bedroom of inner memories,
Of illness and intermittent happiness.
Autumn is evident in the garden beds,
Rain on Michaelmas daisies, the lemon-gold
Of leaves and bedraggled flowers.
And it is All Souls' Day, when we pray
For those who were here before us and felt
Perhaps as I do today. A bell tolls
Its melancholy note: Remember them,
The souls of the faithful departed
Who once lived here and had their being
Even as I. The door clangs behind me –

I could tell its sound a hundred miles away;
My feet recall the tread of the stone stairs:
I could find my way blindfold
Who now go down for the last time
And out of the door, for ever, away.

Summoned by Bells

Two ghosts stood talking in the Turl –
'And are we dead?' said one to the other:
'So many of those we knew and loved,
Were young with, are.' 'Perhaps we are, brother.'

At that the bells rang out, over the roofs
And down the street, into the heart
To remind them their friends were not forgot,
Their lives caught up in the tongues

They knew when they were alive and heard them
Just as we, meeting in the street years after,
Were speaking of their endearing ways,
Carefree youth and happy laughter;

How one, though given to malice, was concerned,
When his friend was ill, lest he should die;
How another he loved could not respond,
Yet treasured his letters now too late.

'Too late, too late': these were the words the changes rang
Like fate, all down the scale, and in and out
As those two survivors stood and talked
On the worn pavement, where they had walked

When they were young: recalling their friends,
Their years summoned up so vividly
That which were the dead and which alive
They hardly knew in that moment of mystery.

The Road to Stratford

How well I know the loved, familiar road
   Across the Cotswolds, over the divide
At Great Rollright, the standing stones he knew –
The folklore king and queen holding their court –
And down into the rich Vale of the Red Horse.
I think of him spurring his tired jade,
Measuring the miles away from his friend.
Here the English names lie like a garland
On signpost and turning – Tredington and Shipton,
Ilmington, Idlicote, Alderminster,
Clifford Chambers with its memory
Of friend and poet, fellow countryman,
Now but a name on a stone monument.

Today, at Welcombe, a blue Umbrian sky
Over green lawns; the valley leads the eye
By willow-drooping lake to white fields
Drifted with daisies; the further distance gold
With buttercups, kingcups and his favourite cowslips.
This is the moment of forget-me-nots and flags,
Of thrushes echoing in the coverts, shouting
From tree to tree, woodpigeons, cuckoo-notes
Thrown across the valley, a chime of birds.
Bees visit and knotted snakes emerge
From winter sleep. A Spring breeze filters
Through the beech-fronds, bends over the long grasses
And daffodil leaves bereft of flowers. Puff-balls
Of white may stand in the hedges, a heavy
Chestnut candelabrum hangs over the lake.

Here and there in the glades the lovers walk –
A tall, fair officer out of the R.A.F.,
Strong-shouldered, lithe, short-sleeved shirt,

Complete with spectacled nondescript on arm
(Sweet lovers love the spring). All afternoon,
Amid the scents and sounds of flowers and insects,
I hear the unhappy music of Falstaff's dream.

Now on Whit Sunday, at Shottery, after the war
The twisting lanes and gardens are all tulips
Red and white, bluebells and yellow arabis,
Clumps of lavender in front of Quyny's cottage.
The slope down from Hathaways' is alive
With the movement of blown trees in shadow: their
    yardland
An orchard now, beehives screened by poplars.
A Whitsun crowd, brought out like insects
By the sun: young men in shorts, on bicycles,
Taking photographs; solitaries, children, dogs;
A mouth-organ plays a sad little tune; American
On bike, back from the Pacific war.
Suddenly a bell rings to church
Across gardens ringing with birdsong.

Beyond Long Compton, Brailes Hill stands up
Above the butter-yellow fields of May.
Alighting from the bus a young soldier
Plants his wallflower wife, like a Madonna
With baby, on suitcase in the village street;
The corner decorated with blue irises,
Lilacs blowing their heads about in the breeze,
Dark blue and purple aubrietia, white candytuft,
The thirsty cups of tulips drink in the sun.
And high above heave of hill – the divide,
In blue of sky a pale ha'penny moon
Looks down upon the road he came and went.

Winter in Stratford Church

THE winter wind rattles in roof and rafter,
   Yet all the townsfolk are in church – needs must.
The morning's milk came frozen home in pail.
A flurry of snow dusts the churchyard path
By the charnel house where he saw his little boy:
'I am afraid, and yet I'll venture it.'
The choir where Canons of the College prayed
Is empty now, boarded up, derelict.
Hear the rain and wind beat dark December,
Loosen the leads, worry the quarried panes
Where once glowed saints in all their coloured glory,
Brasses ripped up, slave to mortal rage.
Late-comers arrive, shuffle along to pew,
Huddle together to keep warm in their own steam
That mingles with smoke of brazier at the back,
Spiralling up into the tower by the font,
Where he and all the family were christened.
Now they are gathered up in front, below
The pulpit where coughing drowns the parson's saw.

Suddenly a word is dropped into that well
Of the imagination, the listening ear:
'Therefore hath he mercy on whom he will
Have mercy, and whom he will he hardeneth.'
The ears that take everything that people say,
Automatically register absurdities,
Shut out the noises of the congregation,
While thoughts stir behind the secret forehead.
'On my frailties why are frailer spies,
Which in their wills think bad what I think good?
No: I am that I am.'
                    The homely wife

Sits unstirred, unobtruding, beside him,
Noticing nothing, no disturbance of mind –
Or how much does she know or guess, who keeps
Silence, never uttering a word?
Remorse of conscience for what cannot now be helped
Enters the crevices, thoughts cohere
While eyes wander around the white-washed walls
That yet not obliterate the Risen Lord
In judgment, the Doom looking on the scene,
The good and bad in everyone, the true
And seeming, the ineradicable fault
In nature. Words from around the Figure
Now but a shadowy outline on the Cross:
'Why, all the souls that were, were forfeit once
And he that might the vantage best have took
Found out the remedy. How would you be
If He, which is the top of Judgment, should
But judge you as you are. O, think on that!'

Stoke Edith

THIS way the Lady Emily came to church,
   'For sixty-seven years a constant worshipper
And generous benefactor to the poor:'
Now a name on a tablet in November sun
Among the ordered Georgian pews – the one
For the family deserted, up by the altar
Where they are gathered in, the line ended.
One has the sense the place is not attended
As when the Lady Emily lived on in state,
A widow in her weeds for half a century.
See the grateful poor from the cottages
At church on Sundays – their pale faces press
Against the yew hedge that's still in shape,
Though overgrown with ivy, laced with elder.
A little frost in the carriage-way – one might
Still think the print of horses' hooves; at night
She would command the carriage for so short a drive.

Here is no mystery to penetrate,
No superfluous spiritual illumination,
As at Burnt Norton or Little Gidding, only
The loss of money, failure of a family –
As if that is not mysterious enough,
That one generation should be able to create
And build, and then the vital spark give out,
Flicker feebly for a while, then go quite out.
Leaving this hole in the sky where a great house was
With its eager life, the footmen pursuing the maids,
The stables full of hunters and carriage-horses,
Saddles and harness bright as battering sandal;
Portly butler at the front door where I stand
In vacant space; the oval that was lawn

Still there untrimmed, awaiting the carriages
For Sunday church or a neighbourly visit.
In the stable wing a trapped bird beats itself
Against the glass. The garden is waiting there,
Overgrown with old man's beard and spindle,
Shadowed by cedars looming darkly down
On the ruin and devastation, where all was order,
The paths prim and swept, the lawns razored;
The hounds and hunters gathered for a meet,
The family assembled for welcome or farewell.
I am the only visitor, a man
Dedicated to remembering such things,
To recovering the irrecoverable,
Gathering the fragments to shore up our ruin,
Nourish the shadows no one cares to think of,
Cherish the ghosts to give them a little warmth,
A local habitation and a name.

The Squire of Felbrigg

GATHER these fragments from my friend's life,
Rounded and finished, returned to the soil
He loved, woodlands and fields of Norfolk,
The belt of trees the forbears planted
Between Felbrigg and the sea.
Here the boy at Harrow hears
The wild duck winging over the house at Beeston,
Smells the fresh air from the sea, yet flower-
Scented from the garden. Here's his bird
That sang through months of illness and winter
To cheer him. Here is his golden retriever,
Ruby, with the master in the woods all day,
The peopled trees he loved, squirrel, finch, thrush –
Though more for themselves, for their upthrust
To the skies, the spareness of silver birch,
The strength of ribbed oak, the wonder and worship
Of woods, spread with bluebells in spring,
In autumn carpeted with fern.
Summers in Le Fayet and Chamonix,
Lucky boy, already familiar with antique shops,
Mezzotints and lacquer trays,
Knew the blue of Tibetan poppies.
Your brother dead, you became my friend:
Now dead in turn, my junior in years,
I find these fragments of your early life
I did not know,
Piece together the portrait of what you were
Near fifty years ago.

Sunday Afternoon in Hartford, Conn.

SITTING in the sober shaded light
  Of this New England house on Sunday afternoon,
Blinds half-drawn to exclude the sun
Of the Indian summer, while an English sparrow
Scrattles along the chaste birch boughs
Soon to be stripped by winter snows,
I think of you, dear Tom, dear T.S.E.,
With sudden unexpected poignancy,
Of whom I had not thought so feelingly
Since that day along the Los Angeles Crest Highway
I heard of your death, and wept to be
So far away from home, fancied I could hear
The sound of church bells ringing for you
At East Coker, in the silence of the mountains,
And felt their aching void, ridge beyond ridge.

Now here's a bridge to you, your own New England:
The strangeness of a foreign land falls away,
And I feel more at home for the thought of you,
In this familiar Longfellow house upon the avenue,
Where your aunt, Miss Helen Slingsby, might have lived –
The outlook from the porch across grass verge
To juniper and sumach behind white palings,
To the park where gingko, maple and bog-oak
Jostle marsh-cypress, white pine and many a conifer,
I look upon your book, and read your life,
Look once more into your eye, limpid and sad.
Note the old expression at once severe and gay,
Diffidence and kindness in your anxious smile.

Elizabeth Park

ALONG Prospect Avenue, the cars speed by
Like sizzling water, by Faith Center
And the Seventh Day Adventist Church
('I'm sorry, but we don't approve of tea.')
Dogs bark domestically
By redberried dogwood and yellow sycamore,
Where squirrels chatter and jays call;
So past redbrick condominium into the park.

Here in Elizabeth Park, where the maples turn,
October sun, I look down the slope
To Hartford, Insurance capital of the U.S.A.:
Grandly the towers rise of the Travellers,
The Aetna, and the Hartford Fire Insurance Company,
Hardly distinguishable from St Joseph's Cathedral
Of an earlier form of faith.
The young men exercise their bodies –
All they have to offer – with a ball,
The infantile cult of youth.
A grey-haired, middle-aged man
Sprints vacuously round and round the park
In widening circles, a pebble in a pond –
While I, for all the sun and flaming foliage,
Feel not at home, for ever outside:
An alien wherever I may be.

Chick Austin

SEVENTEEN years since you vanished from the scene
  You set, where we are all gathered in your absence:
'The paste-board palace', the Philistines called
Your creation; others 'the stage set' – which it was:
The background to your works and days,
Where you played your pranks, acted out
The drama of your life, 'Hamlet' to your self –
– Reflecting mirror, rather than to stupid others:
The narcissist in love with himself, for whose
Faithless charm the others fell but not understood.
From an older, more tolerant, understanding world
You brought back notions to this Puritan reef,
Conventional, conformist, Congregational,
Of Everetts, Hales and Goodwins, among whom you
    married –
The pro-cathedral in Paris, honeymoon over the Alps,
Harefoot over the moon, Palladio, Vicenza;
The villa on the Brenta lived again in you.
The formal avenue leads to the Venetian front,
Within, the steep curved staircase, breakneck
Like your headlong life, the descent into the drawing room
Pannini-panelled, gilt Italian furniture,
Guercino, Ricci, Battoni, the baroque you loved,
The rococo fantasy you lived,
Free as air and as mercurial.
'A museum is where the director is amused:'
The avuncular guardians much disapproved.
Having received your *congé*, taking off
For Sarasota and the gay Gulf, a world away
From Puritan New England of your birth,
Accumulating images of freedom as you went,
Leaving at last houses to the number of seven.

Still finding no haven for your life of dream
And ardour, pursuing the mirage of love
In vain – until at last, stricken still young,
When you came to die you came home to Helen,
Waiting for you in this creation of your mind –
Where I, who never knew you, Chick, remember you:
The dead man more alive to me in all this gathering
Of the phantom living – brought back
To be buried at Windham with your forefathers
A bowshot from the church where you were a boy.

Mississippi Wind

THE wind blows puffs of cotton along the verge,
  The cotton pickers are in the fields, or baling;
Kudzu vines run up the roadside trees,
Tremble in the wind like stage greenery.
Here I am in the querulous, glittering South,
The land of copperheads and red necks,
Where darkies couple under the magnolias.
A stiff wind invigorates after the foetid summer,
Tosses the manes of black walnut and pecan,
Scatters the unripe fruit upon the floor;
While blue jays cry across the countryside,
The blue dome cloudless over all.
This is October: the undersides of leaves
Turn silver in the sun, the pyracanthus
Gleams gold across the level lawn, where birds
Are blown and flutter in the improbable wind.
A negro passes on the path, but does not speak,
Maintains dignity and silence, for this is the South.
This is Mississippi, where they live
Their inner life of inscrutable reserve,
A people apart, the progeny of Ham.

The Stranger at Gettysburg

HERE is Seminary Ridge where they stood
  Those first July days of 1863:
Below the Ridge the Lutheran Seminary
With round cupola from which the generals,
First Union, then Confederate, surveyed the scene.
They used the dormitory as a hospital.
Now it's early Spring, and the mocking bird
Calls chuch-chuck-chuck, sweet-sweet.
Within, the clear sun of Pennsylvania
Comes silvered through chapel windows:
Ein feste Burg ist unser Gott.

Powhattan Artillery and Dance's Battalion
Reached the field at evening to turn their batteries
On Cemetery Hill: the great cannonade
Before Longstreet's assault on the Ridge.
Pickett's Division of Longstreet's Corps,
Marching from Chambersburg, arrived after sunset;
Stuart's Cavalry from Hanover engaged Hampton's
In the summer evening at Hunterstown.
In Shultz Woods guns blazed among rocks and oaks;
Troops concentrating at the end of June,
Converging upon this murderous moment of time.

In the early morning, soldiers bivouacked,
Smoke of breakfast rising among trees;
Lee, thoughtful and calm on 'Traveller':
'If ours were not so bloody a business,
What a wonderful spectacle!'
Ein feste Burg . . .

Line of battle formed on either side the pike,
The McMillan house, high on the ridge, saw all.
Thomas's brigade of Georgia Infantry

Moved across the pike into McMillan Woods.
Crows fly across these peopled solitudes,
Glisten funereal black under the sun.
Meade appeared on Cemetery sky-line,
Where now dead cannon balls gleam and shine.
Ein feste Burg ist unser Gott.

To the west, then in setting sun –
The slopes of South Mountain, now shorn and bare;
Squirrels frolic among the falling shadows.
Here stood North Carolina under command,
Brockenborough, Heth and Pettigrew,
Her regiments in action all through
Those days – one Confederate soldier
In four who fell was a North Carolinian.
All these are English names. A sentinel bird
Is surprised at the stranger in tears
At these men's memorial.

The opposing ridge is a graveyard of monuments –
Two carrion crows fight the battle over again
Across the intervening space. Still
The North Carolina colour-bearer thrusts
His flag forward against a burst of copse;
Still the bugler-boy sounds the assault
For Virginia – looks across to where
The Pennsylvania Centre holds fast.

Oak leaves of winter scatter like paper
Where then the foliage was full on the trees.
Stillness, sun and quiet where so many died.
Big Round Top and Little Round Top
Close the view in the morning haze.

Suddenly a jay rends the silence
With the scream of a wounded man.
The breeze brings balm as there was none
In those hot days of '63, under the sun.

Here the Georgia Infantry broke the Union line
At the Angle – attacked in flank, the Federals
Fought their way out with heavy loss.
A pheasant squawks a comment upon
The Army of Northern Virginia
    against the Army of the Potomac.

From Little Round Top one sees the mountains,
The whole Confederate position screened by woods:
Longstreet's Corps drove back the Union line
Entrenched from Devil's Den to Peach Orchard.
Here Massachusetts held firm amid the boulders,
Where Father William Corby, chaplain of brigade,
Bearded, in long coat, stole over shoulders,
Gave absolution to all men on the field,
Killing each other.
New York Engineers bivouacked by
Hummelbaugh House, bullet holes in the barn,
Where hyacinths now bloom,
The catkins coming out on Culp's Hill;
In the creek the early peepers
Keep up their perpetual whirr.
From Jeb Steuart's monument
A nut-hatch drops, eyes the stranger
Meditating the mingled glory
And idiocy of men.

A broad-shouldered veteran of the late war
Surveys the field with practised eye.

Behind where Maine Infantry stood
Sharp-shooters came round out of the wood.
Young saplings stand erect and straight.
A deer crops here where New York Cavalry
Were halted, eyes the stranger, puts up
A white scut of tail, vanishes into cover.
From Meade's Headquarters Old Glory flies over
Alike the blue and the grey.

Today, a robin chatters among silent guns.
At the crossroads to Hagerstown
The retreat took place, behind breast works
Thrown up along the road to Waynesborough;
And Lee withdrew.

Drifts of dead oak leaves dried in the channels,
The trees begin again to put forth leaf.
A flicker of crimson-headed woodpecker
Crosses the path of the Stranger:
Silence and sun and sadness in the air,
Spring and a hint of Resurrection,
No more.

In Memoriam: E. H.

B EHOLD the brecklands of Norfolk
    this November morning:
Intermittent sun lights up
        a Cotman church-tower like a cup,
Catches the bellies of wood-pigeons in flight
        across ploughland and pale park.
The early sun gleams on the dark
        ivied trees of Old Crome,
Russets the plumage of beech and oak
        over the undulating pastures.
Pheasants strut in the stubble, reflect
        the broken blue skies of Peter de Wint
        in peacock hue upon proud neck
        and tail-feathers arched like the firmament.
Birds collect in formation for winter flight
        while the train shuttles across
        the lighted landscape of ridge and furrow.
And it is All Souls' Day, bright
        as a day shimmers in summer.

In New York it is still night:
An only light glimmers under a green shade
        where a girl lies sleeping,
        a smile upon the clever sensitive lips,
Those lambent eyes closed for ever,
The flower-like face shut up in night,
        a tulip cut upon its slender stalk,
The shapely head fallen to one side,
The light now extinguished quite.

Adam

ALL my life I've always been frustrated
  By envious human beings, inspired by jealousy
Of an evident and honest superiority
(See Milton) at school and at the university,
In literary life, the snake-pit of society:
If they could checkmate, frustrate, keep out,
Reject one already from the hour of birth,
They would, themselves unknowing the inner fact
But intuitively inspired, if they could, to destroy
The growing boy.
In fact, all has worked out very well,
Rid me of any obligation to my kind,
Enabled me to concentrate on the thing in hand,
The assumption being – their loss, not mine.
Quite another thing from the sense of providence
That guided me, the guardian angel at the gate,
Forced me to labour in the sweat of my brow –
Without the distractions of seductive Eve –
At that which from the first I was meant to do.
With split nature, impossible to satisfy,
Gifts on one side, defects on the other
To turn into advantages, eventual triumph –
A pity perhaps – over original good nature
Like Adam's, now become Swift's.
Repent not, nor conciliate: the achievement's
The thing, the ecstasy, the rapture,
Listening alone in the silence for the word,
One apart from others, evening light
On darkening beech and over the threatened city,
Civilisation falling in the sound of bells,
Rising and falling, relishing the thought that
Knowing humans is a waste of time.

The Outsider

OUTSIDE, for ever outside of everywhere,
  Never within the welcoming walls
Where others are at ease and feel at home,
In their familiar aquarium:
Unaware of themselves in their element –
Fish in water, for ever pursuing each other,
Jaws working, gaping and gawping with fixed stare,
Unaware of where or what they are.
Would one be one of those, warm in the tank,
Or prefer to be well outside on one's own,
Alone, but an observant, sentient being,
Without illusions, knowing the human score?

Knowing

'Nobody ever understands anything.' Henry James

Certainty?
Apparently
They object to my certainty:
But what's the point of writing about
What you are not certain about?
Better to keep your uncertainties
To yourself, retain mysteries
Within the inner shaping self
Until they come clear,
Ready for the light of day,
Sharp as a bugle-call.

As for them all
Living in a never-never land
Of doubt and unclarity –
Naturally
They cannot see
Anything defined or clear.
They should be content with what is,
Thankful for small mercies,
Rendered so
For their benefit, to learn
Since they cannot discern
And never know.

The Scillies: Finis Terrae

THE world is uninteresting today:
  Too small and cramped, nowhere
That is not already known –
None of the excitement of early explorers
Finding new islands like rain
Scattered upon the surface of the seas.
Cramped and cabined and confined
We are here in our murderous crevices
Too well informed of every day's news
Of ambushes, traps, bombs in bars,
Too many people, too many everywhere –
More of them arriving every day at Heathrow,
Turbaned, bearded, living in suitcases,
Swathed in bright-coloured saris,
Saffron, canary yellow, lemon or lavender,
Swamping the silly little island
Where the people have never had it so good.
Nowhere for us to go to, nowhere to go:
We must content ourselves with the Scillies.[1]

---

[1] Adopted retreat of Sir Harold Wilson, Knight of the Garter.

On Being Robbed

SOMEWHERE, wide in the world,
  Is an unknown man
Who knows all my intimacies,
Has been through all my things,
My cupboards, closets, cabinets,
Chests of drawers, boxes, desks, papers,
Been into every room, through every thing,
Knows the whole run of my house:
Smashed three windows, forced two doors
To break into this locked and barred redoubt,
Leaving a bloodstain to remember him by.

Now he knows me through and through,
This unknown man two hundred miles away –
No starlight lit his lonesomeness,
Just a few matches thrown about
Here and there, until he found
My phallic torch.

Then all was not difficult – to make away
With delicate blue-john urns, their ormolu swag
Having an allure for this old lag –
Or more likely young. Which was he?
How much I long to see
Him by the light of day.

Unknown prowler while I was away,
I long to see you face to face,
Hug and hold in a thief's embrace.
Mysterious intruder, my life
Has no mystery for you –
All laid bare in my rare possessions,
Snuff-boxes, card-cases, *étuis*,

Porcelain, agate, tortoise-shell, mother-of-pearl,
That have accompanied me over the years
Since I, a boy from the working class
Not far removed from you,
Used to come here and long to enter in –
No thought of shivering the glass –
This lonely paradise, no longer now alone,
For you have penetrated.

Everywhere I look I see you here,
Lurking on staircase, in corners,
Behind curtains, in bedroom and corridor,
A shadow in the night's alarms.
O thug and thief, my robber and lover,
Come forth, take me in your arms!

Modernist Verse

THE verse of Sylvia Plath
    Is too esoteric for me;
And yet there's no doubt at all
    It's authentic poetry.

Her poetry shows very clear
    She was obsessed by suicide
Drug-haunted, dream-tormented,
    Swung by every moon and tide.

Such fine-spun intellectual drift
    He may catch and hold who can:
Verse so exotic can never speak
    Clearly to the heart of man.

Children's Verses

The Rooks at Trenarren

WHEN the rooks descry me
'Caw-Caw-Caw' they say,
In the morning quiet
At the dawn of day,

When I go out at door
To unbar the outer gate,
And up the unswept gravel –
Whether I'm early or late

'Caw-Caw-Caw' they say,
Sending the message round,
Giving the alert
With their barbaric sound –

As if I'm an interloper
In this ancient place,
Where they for generations
Had bred their corvine race.

They took a sudden fancy,
After many a year,
To build their noisy nests
Upon the treetops here.

They chose the common conifers
With their ragged line,
Ignoring beech and chestnut
And the great insignis pine.

No children in the house –
The rooks all fly away,
Desert their lofty nests,
So the old folks say.

This year they're back again –
And what does that portend?
A prolific year for poems,
The children of the mind?

A raucous row they keep,
Building their nests on high,
Rearing their silent young,
With many a warning cry,

Teach them to leave their nests,
Encourage them to fly –
Till, on a summer morning
With lyric ecstasy,
Out they sail their black ships
Across the waiting sky.

Charlestown Church Bells

Noel, Piran, Petroc,
        Michael, Morwenna, Paul,
To the church above the harbour
        Sweet and silvery call.

They send their message outward
        Across the crystal bay,
And bless the passing seasons
        From New Year to Christmas Day.

Ring out around the coast line
        From the Gribbin to Black Head
Summoning the living,
        Remembering the dead.

Who once lived in these places,
        Porthpean, Charlestown, Duporth,
The miners of Wheal Eliza,
        The farmers of Kilmarth;

And inland to Tregrehan,
        Along the sands of Par,
At morning and at evening
        They send their message far

To remoter Menabilly,
        The grey quay of Polkerris
Under its grove of trees,
        And over the cliffs to Crinnis:

Speaking their living language
        Alike to the quick and the dead,
For all are one communion
        For whom Christ's blood was shed.

These are his saints they're named for,
    With one who answered their call:[1]
Noel, Piran, Petroc,
    Michael, Morwenna, Paul.

[1] Noel Coward, who loved Charlestown, gave the bell named for him.

The Pleasant Places of Devon

Do you know Maristow,
    Bridestowe or Virginstow?
O come to Brimmacombe,
Dunchideock or Challacombe,
Broadswoodwidger, Tetcott,
Ellacott or Priestacott.
Though we've no Toller Porcorum
There's Buckland and Zeal Monachorum.
From Thrushelton and Kelly
Take the turning to Bratton Clovelly;
Nor is it far to seek
Germansweek or Bramford Speke.
We're contented here
With Larkbeare or Rockbeare;
All is very well
At Sampford Peverel or Sydenham Damerel.
Come to Dittisham in cherry time
Or Gittisham at any time
O Lovadon and Livaton,
Caddaford and Baddaford,
St Giles-in-the-Heath and Strete
Are very hard to beat.
Shuttaford and Shallowford,
Harford and Bittaford,
Owl's Rattle and Rattery,
Woolfardisworthy[1] and Ottery,
Doddiscomleigh and Throwleigh –
Through which you must drive slowly,
The road is so narrow,
As at Ugborough or White Barrow –
Petertavy and Marytavy

[1] Pronounced Woolsery.

Are surely,
With Cruys Morchard
And Whimple with its cider orchard,
Torbryan and then
Sampford Courtenay and Ipplepen,
Sampford Spiney and Manaton,
Bagtor and Ilsington
Broadclyst and Clyst Honiton,
Lamerton or Coryton,
Collacombe or Hayne,
The pleasantest places
In sun
Or rain.

Apollo, Glorious Labrador

for Harold and Joan Hartley

A POLLO, glorious labrador,
   Of golden coat and amber eyes,
Of your regal looks and gentle ways
We have so many memories.

What a kingdom you had here:
Trevissick Turn to Hallane Mill,
Trenarren village and Ropehawn,
Along the headland to flagstaff hill.

All the beaches here were yours,
Porthtowan, Gwendra, Silvermine,
When you were young and frolicsome,
In summer days, of sheen or shine.

Following your master into the sea,
Close on his track, treading the waves,
Bounding across seaweed and rocks,
Under the Vans, exploring the caves.

You toss your treasure trove in the air,
Flotsam and jetsam, wrack of the sea,
Pieces of spar, a cellophane square
To protect from the birds his cherry tree.

What days you had of bliss and joy
Splashing in the valley stream;
Back to the shelter of Rose Cottage
All the night, perchance to dream

How once you chased my favourite cat;
Peter, the white Persian, spat
Fury from the safety of a tree

At such a breach of his dignity:
Nor was I wholly pleased thereat –

But forgave you for your charming way
Of welcoming me, a visitor,
With a present of your bone or toy,
A shoe or slipper at your door.
You became with advancing age
A wise old dog, a sober sage,
Couchant before the friendly fire
Of the ever hospitable squire

Who made Rose Cottage what it is –
A haven of all felicities.
How much we miss you: there's not much fun
At your home now you are gone.
Yet, on reflection, I am glad
To think what a golden life you had.

Retiring to Cornwall

R ETIRING to Cornwall
 You can always play games
With odd Cornish names:
For example, there's ample
Room to ramble
At Chapel Amble.
Do you feel a hunger
To live at St Ingunger,
Or would you prefer Tresunger?
Or a positive ache
For a quiet life at Landrake?
Would you quake
At the thought of a journey
With a forgetful attorney
To remote St Erney?
If so,
Consider Davidstow,
Or moorland Michaelstow,
Petrockstow or Perranzabuloe.
Express no scorn
For Ruan Lanihorne
Of Epaphroditus, former vicar, all forlorn.
You could do worse than put
Your funds into a house at Herodsfoot,
A roadside stall at Trerulefoot;
Or share a boat with a boy-
Friend at Fowey,
With a nice ingle-nook at 'The Ship-Ahoy'.
Do not join the blimps
Or hope to catch shrimps
At Ventongimps.
You might have reason for ruth

To leave a good thing at Redruth
In hopes of a better at Ponsanooth;
One might well feel lazy,
Or at least a little crazy
At demotic St Blazey,
While the crowds at Mevagissey[1]
Are enough to make one dizzy –
Better retire to inland St Issey.
You could take a boat from Polruan
And cautiously ribbon
Around Point Gribben
To land at Pentewan.
Just as one arrives
To take a lease for three lives,
In the old Cornish manner, at St Ives:
But abstain from three wives –
Nor take one at all
In the parish of Paul,
Better to catch lobsters off Prawle.
What kind of a dance
Would you lead at Penzance?
You could prance practically to Kynance,
Or, replete with Cornwall, retreat to France.

[1] The proper pronunciation is Mevagizzey and St Izzey: these Cornish
's's are 'z's.